By Grace of G-D

DIVINE IMAGE

Insights into the Noahide Laws

Adapted by

Rabbi Yakov David Cohen

ISBN: 1-5057-8243-0   978-1-5057-8243-1

Published by the Institute of Noahide Code

A United Nations (UN NGO ECOSOC)

www.Noahide.org

Printed in the United States of America

CONTENTS

INTRODUCTION

E very person is created with a Divine image. It is the task of every one of us to elevate all human activity to a Divine purpose. In short, this means being able to connect every human activity with G-d - and this is precisely the purpose of the Torah and its commandments, called mitzvoth in Hebrew. Every human being has the unique ability to connect his entire being with the Creator. Upon achieving this task, he creates a dwelling place for G-d in this world, thereby fulfilling the purpose of creation.

As is explained in this book, the worlds of the spiritual and the physical are not in conflict. Their ultimate purpose is that they be fused-together with the physical being permeated by the spiritual. The core element of every mitzvah - commandment performance is to take the physical creation and utilize it for the Divine purpose. Thereby achieving a wonderful harmony both in the individual and in the world at large. This is a theme that encompasses all times and places; wherever and whenever a person operates, he is able to utilize the task at hand for its correct and Divine purpose, thus transforming the world into a dwelling place for G-d.

Every human being, is, to borrow the biblical phrase, "created in the image of G-d", and thus fit to "imitate G-d", - an imitation pertinent to all humankind, but which can only take place through the performance of the Divinely given commandments.

There are seven laws, which are biblically binding on all humanity. They include prohibitions on idolatry, blasphemy or the reviling of G-d, forbidden sexual relationships, theft, murder, lawlessness, e.g. the failure to establish courts with the ability to enforce justice and cruelty to animals. These are known as the Seven Noahide Laws.

The reason for the name 'Noahide', is that although the first six of these laws were originally commanded to the first person, Adam, the seven laws were completed with Noah, to whom the seventh commandment was given. Only after the Flood, was mankind permitted to slaughter meat for consumption, and with this came the law prohibiting one to 'eat the limb of a living animal' and treating them cruelly.

The seven laws of Noah form a base with many ramifications, from which many more Mitzvoth-commandments given by G-d Almighty to Moses on Mt. Sinai to transmit to all nations of the world, the reader is encouraged to learn more by asking questions and studying Torah, in particular the insights in the Jewish Chasiddus Chabad - philosophy, upon which many of the concepts are discussed in this book.

Rabbi Menachem Mendel Schneerson, the leader of the Chabad, Lubavitch worldwide Jewish movement, stated that the observance of Noahide Laws by all humankind will be a principle force bring about Universal Peace and the Messianic Redemption.

The Rebbe explained that the basic nature of our world is perfect and good, our every good action is real and enduring, while every negative action is just that – an unreal negative phenomenon, a void waiting to be dispelled. Hence, the common equation of evil with darkness and good with light. Darkness, no matter how threatening and intimidating, is merely the absence of light. Light need not combat and overpower darkness in order to displace it -- where light is, darkness is not. A thimbleful of light will therefore banish a roomful of darkness.

Rabbi Yakov David Cohen

Founder / Director Institute of Noahide Code – www.Noahide.org

New York, NY USA

ACKNOWLEDGEMENTS

With gratitude to the G-d Almighty for the privilege of bringing knowledge of the Creator's wisdom and purpose for mankind and disseminating the teachings of Torah and Chassidut to all people.

This book collects a number of articles written by a variety of writers and lecturers over the years. These works came to explain general concepts in Chabad philosophy and were adopted here to address the laws of Noah for all people. Many thanks to the following Rabbis and scholar: Boruch S Jacobson and Shimon D Cowen and Betzalel Malasky. The reader is encouraged to read the complete and other pertinent articles on spirituality and purpose.

These essays do not claim to present or imply authoritative Jewish Legal rulings known as Halachah. For those and for guidance as to what one may observe, one must consult an orthodox Rabbi, for guidance in the Noahide laws and their observance.

It is the fundamental belief that all humankind is created in the Divine Image. As Rabbi Isracl Baal Shem Tov asked "When will Moshiach- messiah come? The answer he received "when the wellsprings of your Torah will be disseminated". It is the hope that this inborn Divine Image will encourage the reader to fulfil the Noahide laws and to learn more about the Divine purpose of making the world a dwelling place for G-d, thus hastening the era of Moshiach (Messiah).

which he became ruler over the entire creation. All the creatures gathered to serve him and to crown him as their creator. But Adam, pointing out their error, said to them, "Let us all come and worship G-d our Maker" The "world conquest", given to the human as his task and mission in life, was to elevate and refine the whole of nature, including the beasts and animals, to the service of true humanity; a humanity which is permeated and illuminated by the Divine Image - by the soul, so that the whole of creation will realize, that G-d is the Creator of all. The Torah is the blueprint for everyone and every thing in this world.

Needless to say, before a human being sets out to conquer the world he must first conquer himself and his own ego through the subjugation of the "earthly" and the "beastly" element and forces in his own nature. This is attained through actions which are in accord with the directives of the Torah - the practical guide to everyday living so that the material world becomes permeated and illuminated with the light of the One Almighty G-d.

In the beginning G-d created one man, and upon this single person on earth, He imposed this duty and task. Herein lies the profound yet clear directive, namely, that each and every person, is potentially capable of "conquering the world". If a person does not fulfill his task and does not utilize his inestimable Divine powers, it is not merely a personal loss and failure for him, but also something that affects the destiny of the whole world.

CAN ONE PERSON CHANGE THE WORLD?

One of the main distinguishing features in the creation of man is that man was created as a single being, unlike other species which were created in large numbers.

This indicates emphatically that one single individual has the capacity to bring the whole of creation to fulfillment, as was the case with the first man, Adam. No sooner was Adam created, than he called upon and rallied all the creatures in the world to recognize the sovereignty of the Creator with 'the cry, "Come, let-us prostrate ourselves, let us bow down and kneel before G-d our Maker". For it is only through self- abnegation that a created being can attach itself to, and be united with, the Creator and thus attain fulfillment of the highest order.

The Rabbis teach us, that Adam was the prototype and example for each and every individual to follow. "For this reason was man created single, in order to teach us that 'one person is equivalent to an entire world' ". This means that every human being; regardless of time and place and personal status, has the fullest capacity, and also the duty, to rise and attain the highest degree of fulfillment, and accomplish the same for creation as a whole.

G-D IS ALL AND EVERYTHING IS G-D

As expressed by Maimonides "The foundation of all foundations, and the pillar of all wisdom, is to know that there is a First Existence, who brings all existences into being" - opening to Code of Law

One must believe that there is an eye that sees and an ear that hears. By definition believing is to accept G-d as a reality in our life and Him to be. The way each one of us perceives G-d will depend largely on our perception from childhood and/or our current influences.

Can the existence of G-d be proven? In truth we must analyze the question before we attempt an answer. What is considered a proof? How does one prove that anything exists? Take for example, a blind man. Do colors exist for the blind man? He cannot see colors, yet they still exist that fact is established by others who can see. The blind man believes and trusts that his fellow men can see that colors do exist although it is beyond his personal experience: For a further example, take electricity. When we turn on a light, can we see electricity? The answer is no, we see only its effect. Take gravity. When an object falls we cannot see, hear, feel, taste or smell gravity - we only see its effect. All will agree that gravity is an undisputed fact of nature since we see its effect. Scientists today are still baffled as to exactly what is the "stuff" of gravity. In short, the proof of existence of any matter does not necessarily mean that we have to sense it in any way. It exists because we see its effect.

THE POWER OF THE RIGHTEOUS.

Immediately after the creation, the Biblical story continues with the temptation of the forbidden fruit, Adam and Eve's sin and the subsequent exile from the Garden of Eden. The snake, synonymous with evil inclinations, persuades man to disregard the mission of his soul in return for momentary pleasure. Adam plunged mankind into a constant struggle between the good and evil inclinations (in Hebrew Yezertov and Yezerhara). The Torah describes what happened in the following way: At the time of creation, the Shechinah, or Divine Presence, rested on earth. After the sin of Adam the Shechinah removed itself from the earth.

There were ten generations from Adam to Noah. This long era of humanity was a history of deterioration and removal of the Divine image from humankind. Noah was unable to save or redeem the increasing decadence of these generations: his shining ark was the refuge of the *ideal* of a redeemed humankind and nature. Another ten generations passed from Noah to Abraham. While both intervals of ten generations are part of what the Torah called the two thousand years of void or *Tohu,* meaning spiritual darkness, Abraham's relationship to the era which preceded him was different.   He was able to redeem the historical era of the ten generations, which preceded him.

This was because the service of Abraham marked the beginning of a new era in humanity, called the "two thousand years of Torah-- Divine teaching". Torah is associated with "light", symbolizing clear and manifest G-dly truth. Just as the Torah through its commandments formed the instrument of the refinement of the world, so Abraham, having realized the unity consciousness of the One Creator in the fullness for himself at the age of 3 thereby becomes the father of monotheism, and then worked on uplifting the human environment around him. In the process, he himself practiced and spread the observance of the basic spiritual laws of humanity known as the Noahide laws or Seven laws of Noah, starting with the recognition of the unity of Al-mighty G-d, as well as keeping a further commandment, circumcision, which was given to him and forms the bridge to the further group of commandments incumbent on the Jewish people, to be given later at Mt. Sinai i.e. the 613, in contrast to, but including in them, the Noahide laws incumbent upon all humanity. In this sense Abraham was already a Noahide, but he was also the father of the Jewish people with their own distinct spiritual character and task and responsibility. In his offspring, Yitzhak and Ishmael and his grandsons Yakov and Esau, the partnership between the families of nations is born, where Jew and gentile, with their complementary tasks build a dwelling place for the revealed presence of the Creator.

These laws are a basic "possession" of humanity. For the human being is, to use the biblical phrase, "Created in the Image of G-d", that is to say, enabled to "Imitate G-d", and this imitation can take place only through the performance of the Divinely given Noahide commandments. The reason for this is because these laws help the person respect the Creator and his merciful and just ways.

One of the great teachings of Rabbi Baal Shem Tov 1698-1760, the founder of the Chassidic movement, is that there is not a one-time creation but rather an ongoing creative process. Divine creative energy is constantly pulsating through creation, bringing it into being *ex nihilo* (from nothing) every single second. If G-d were to stop creating the world, even for an instant, it would revert to null and void, as before the creation. When the Torah talks about the idea of a "removal of the Divine Presence", they are not suggesting that G-d literally removed Himself from the world; otherwise the world would cease to exist. Rather they are suggesting that sin creates an insensitivity to that Divine Presence in human beings. G-liness is no longer manifest and felt by creation. It is almost as though G-d is in exile from His own world. This was the result of the generations of sin and it was only through the efforts of the righteous that the world can again be sensitized to the Divine Presence and become a fitting dwelling place for His presence.

GOOD AND EVIL

The Torah metaphor for evil is darkness-an absence of light which, not unlike the absence of truth, is aught but a void of reality. Like darkness, evil has no power of its own. From where, then, does it derive the power to cause so much pain in the world?

In the beginning, Adam and Eve could have simply ignored it and it would have eventually dissolved into the sparks of G-dly light they revealed in the Garden. However once evil has been fed and lives out of its bag, it can never be dealt with so smoothly again.

Nevertheless, our major weapon against evil is to add light by focusing on good. This is perhaps the Lubavitcher Rebbe's most common response to those who wrote asking for counsel to deal with the evil in their daily lives -- whether it be anger, temptation, disturbing thoughts, bad dreams, over and over, the Rebbe writes, "Do more good and remove your mind from the issue." Even in matters of health, the Rebbe advised, "Find a good doctor, who will be concerned with your problems. Then simply follow his instructions and remove your mind from the sickness."

On a global scale, evil is not something to fear, much less to negotiate with. That only gives it more power. Yes, there are times when you have no choice but to battle evil -- as the Maccabees did against the Syrian-Greek oppressor. But stoop to conquer evil and you will only join it in its mud. Against evil, you must march to battle on the clouds. You must trample it, while never looking down. On the contrary, while in battle against evil, you must find yourself reaching higher and higher.

That is why it is so important today for us to create more light. Even a little light pushes away a lot of darkness. For every shadow of darkness we see, we must produce megawatts of blinding light. In fact, this is the purpose of evil, why a G-d who is entirely good, devised evil to be in His world. Because evil forces us to reach deep inside, to find our inner strength, climbing ever higher, until reaching a brilliant, blinding light -- a light that leaves no crevice for darkness to hide.

Against that light, evil melts in surrender, having fulfilled its purpose of being. For, in the beginning, darkness was made with a single intent: To squeeze out the inner light of the human soul. A light that knows no bounds. Fight evil with beauty. Defy darkness with infinite light.

WHAT DO I DO?

Every person is created with a Divine image. It is the task of every one of us to elevate all human activity to a Divine purpose. In short, this means being able to connect every human activity with G-d - and this is precisely the purpose of the Torah and its commandments. A human being has the ability to connect his entire being with G-d. Upon achieving this task, he creates a dwelling place for G-d in this world, hence fulfilling the purpose of creation.

The worlds of the spiritual and the physical are not in conflict. The ultimate purpose is that they be fused and the physical permeated with the spiritual, the core of all the commandments performance is to take the physical creation and utilize it for a Divine purpose. This achieves a wonderful harmony both in the individual and in the world at large. This theme is to be encompassed at all times and places; wherever and whenever a person operates, he is able to utilize the task at hand for its correct, Divine purpose, a dwelling place for G-d.

Therefore we must always be aware of our responsibility to the Creator of life and live in His image. And not to serve false gods, money, power and so on and not to accept these concepts as the one and only force that gives life to all. However, living with His presence we bring down Divine light and Presence into this world.

We would do well to heed the advice of King Solomon, the wisest of all men, when he wrote at the end of the book of Ecclesiastes, 'Ultimately, all is known; fear G.-d, and observe His commandments; for this is the whole purpose of man. In the words of our Torah, "I was created for the sole purpose of serving my Maker."

The Seven Noahide Laws demonstrate that the Almighty G-d has rules and laws for all human beings ...and that G-d loves us all. He does not leave anyone, Jew or non-Jew without guidance. To the non-Jew, He has given the Seven Noahide Commandments. Maimonides states "Whoever among the Nations fulfills the Seven Commandments to serve G-d belongs to the Righteous among the Nations, and has his share in the World to Come". Although there are many reasons for a non-Jew to follow the Noahide Laws- because one finds them moral or they appeal to his intellect or his sense of justice- in order to become a Ben Noah, Child of Noah, one must follow these laws, essentially, because he recognizes that they were revealed by G-d, Hashem through Moses to the children of Israel at Mount Sinai.

"One must always perceive the good and evil in oneself and in the world as if in perfect balance. Through doing one good deed, one can tip the scales in favor of the good and bring salvation to oneself and to the entire world." Maimonides.

Each and every one of us carries the enormous responsibility and has the distinct privilege to tip the entire world towards redemption, thereby changing the world for ever.

A central belief in Judaism is the sanctity of life in fact we disregard the Torah in order to save a life, and how every single person on the planet is unique, special, and part of the master plan.

The Rebbe, Rabbi Menachem Mendel Schneerson, leader of the Chabad, Lubavitch world Jewish movement, stated that the Noahide Laws observance by all humankind will bring about universal peace and the Messianic Redemption. The Rebbe explained because the basic nature of our world is perfect and good, our every good action is real and enduring, while every negative action is just that -- a negative phenomenon, a void waiting to be dispelled. Hence, the common equation of evil with darkness and good with light. Darkness, no matter how threatening and intimidating, is merely the absence of light. Light need not combat and overpower darkness in order to displace it -- where light is, darkness is not. A thimbleful of light will therefore banish a roomful of darkness.

HERE ARE SOME POINTS TO PONDER

How do we define G-d?

What do we mean human were created singular?

What does the Torah mean "In the divine image"?

When we say one must first conquer himself and his own ego through the subjugation of the "earthly" and "beastly" in his own nature, what dose that mean?

Belief, Can we prove G-d? Why is it impossible to comprehend G-d?

What is life's purpose? What do I do?

Good and evil – light and darkness, a bit light dispels much darkness.

CHAPTER - LAW 2

RESPECT AND PRAISE OF G-D - DO NOT BLASPHEME HIS NAME

G-d is called the thing of things and ruler of ruler. He is the basis for all that we value, and esteem. Once you recognize G-d as the creator of all, do not be disrespectful to G-d. This means that you must not curse G-d's name. It also implies that you should not use G-d's name disrespectfully. In order to develop proper respect for the Creator, let us think of the respect afforded on earth to royalty.

Imagine that you are in the presence of a great king. Imagine how much respect you would have every time, you pronounced the king's name. You should have even more respect every time you pronounce the name of the King of Kings. Furthermore, you must also learn to respect G-d's judgment. No matter what happens, never complain: and this is the hardest test. Many people as they go through bitter and harsh experiences in life like a car accident, illness, divorces, betrayal and disappointments may begin to develop anger towards G-d. Even though this anger is really only the cover for their hurts, nonetheless they feel that they would like to criticize and complain to G-d. The way out of this is to remember, G-d is good; G-d is the greatest good that exists. There is no other good than G-d-all good thing things we know and experience are actually from G-d. One may not use G-d's name in vain by swearing falsely in positive terms, this entails showing gratitude for the life that we have from the Creator of all life, thanking and blessing G-d. What does it mean to respect G-d? Living in the Divine is loving as G-d loves, Child following in his parent footsteps... which is giving the gift of love unconditionally.

WHAT IS PRAYER?

Correspondence between the Physical and the Spiritual

In Jewish philosophy, nothing is without its purpose in the scheme of things, and no action is devoid of consequences. All words, thoughts and actions have cosmic effect, leading to an increase or decrease of spirituality. Thereby, there is a correct and incorrect way for each action, each pattern of words, and thoughts. That is to say, the entire world is an organic whole and the physical representation of the spiritual realm. Physical action affects the spiritual realm, while in turn spiritual accomplishments affect the physical realm.

By spiritually improving ourselves and interacting with the physical world in a way that increases the corresponding properties of the spiritual world, we in turn influence the entire physical cosmos. Every gain in the spiritual realm causes greater harmony in the physical realm.

We live in a physical universe which is really just a shadow of the "real thing": the spiritual cosmos. We are given the ability to manipulate the spiritual cosmos and to bring it to perfection through our physical action, words and thought. Living in the shadows as we do, we cannot always understand what the purpose of our shadow actions and words is. However, they are as crucial to our wellbeing as to the wellbeing of the cosmos: only our real selves, our spiritual aspect e.g. our souls, can comprehend their true meaning.

Prayer. Every morning, G-d waits for us to pray, but we often don't perform this service with proper intention. If we delay our prayers, they must reflect proper preparation.

When we bless a friend, we wish him success. Can we do the same towards G-d? Does G-d lack something that our prayers can satisfy?

Become close to the Creator of the world. Not only do we thank G-d for His kindness by making a blessing, we are also elevated to a higher level of spiritual awareness.

The visiting rabbi used the blessing to thank G-d for His material blessings, which is commendable. But Rabbi Elimelech used the blessing to connect to G-d. The apple was merely a medium for this.

When the opportunity arises to make a blessing, we too can use it to increase our spiritual awareness. The more prayers and blessings that we make, the more we increase our awareness. That's the point of making a blessing. It is as if we do something for G-d; we bring Him here on earth instead of relegating Him to the heavens.

WHY DO WE PRAY?

Because the body needs the soul and the soul needs the body, and both need to be made aware, that the other's need is also their own. That ultimately is the essence of prayer: to know our needs, to understand their source, and to comprehend their true objectives. To direct our minds and hearts to Him who implanted these needs within us, defined their purpose, and provides us with the means to fulfill them.

The whole concept of praying is confusing. We trust in G-d that He is good and does everything for the good. We believe that He has perfect knowledge of everything and that everything is under His control. At the same time we ask Him to change things and make them good as we understand it. Yes, it seems a contradiction.

So think of it like this: G-d wants people to pray to Him. It is somewhat like a parent want in a child to pick up the phone and say, "Hi, Mom and Dad." More than that, He wants things to progress in His world through mutual consultation and coordination. He wants that we should be involved in understanding what's good for us and in then bringing this good about -- no matter how much better His own understanding and ability is than our understanding and ability.

That's what prayer is all about: Communion between you and G-d literally. Think of prayer as G-d talking to Himself - through you. In prayer, you and G-d are one. Today people hold meetings for business and social causes coming to G-d- in prayer is having a meeting with the Creator. Make a standing appointment and discuss all your plans with Him.

PRAYING WITH A HEART

There a story told about praying with the heart. Once the Rabbi said "G-d loves a heart", a simple person understood this literally and every week he would place a heart in the holy ark inside the synagogue alongside the holy Torah, after many weeks the Rabbi hid and waited to see, who was placing a heart into the holy ark, sure enough Aaron came in ... the Rabbi then explained G-d wants **our** hearts...

BLESSING AND CURSE

"See "I give you today blessing and curse" (Deuteronomy 11:26)."Blessing" is a very important word. We need to know that there is goodness in the world and that this goodness has been given to us and made accessible to us.

"Curse" is an important word, too. We need to know that there are negative things we must reject and defeat. That's what being a moral creature all is about: knowing that there is good and there is bad, knowing to distinguish the one from the other, and knowing to embrace the former and reject the latter. "You" is a very important word, too. You must know that the choice is yours, that you, alone, are responsible for your choices. That the world has been placed in your hearts, and in your hands.

"Today" is also important. Our actions are not a stab in the dark, noted in the depths of Heaven by an invisible G-d, to be accounted for in a distant afterlife. The implications of our choices are present and immediate.

But the most important word in the above-quoted verse is the three letter verb that opens the sentence -- and opens the Torah section of Re'eh (Deuteronomy 11:26-16:17) giving the Parshah its name. It is the word "see".

Of all your senses and faculties, sight is the most real and absolute. Hence the law (Talmud, Rosh Hashanah 27a) that "a witness cannot be a judge." A judge must be open to arguments in defense of the accused; having seen the act committed, this would-be judge has too powerful an impression of the man's guilt -- he is no longer capable of finding sympathy or justification for the deed.

When you hear something, smell something, feel something or deduce something logically, you know it to be true. But this is never an absolute knowledge. There always remains some reservation, some inkling of doubt, some vestige of "yes, but...." But not when something is seen. Thus sight is the "perfect experience" or seeing is believing.

That is why the prophets describe the messianic era as a time of seeing: "Your eyes will see your Master" (Isaiah 30:20); "All flesh will together see that the mouth of G-d has spoken" (ibid. 40:5). To "see" is to inhabit a world in its ultimate state of perfection, a world which has realized its Divine purpose and attained a total and absolute knowledge of its Creator. Since the main object of our sight will be G-dliness itself then. Our perception will be elevated to spiritual perception.

Thus the Torah proclaims: "See, I give you today blessing and curse."

See the blessing. Gain intimate, absolute knowledge of the essential goodness of your Creator, your world, your own soul. It is there; see it.

See the curse. See that it is not truly accursed, for evil is a nonentity, a mere absence as darkness is but a withdrawal of light. See that it "exists" only to challenge you to defeat it, only to provoke your passion for good, only to rouse your most profound loyalties and convictions and powers. See it for what it really isn't and you shall conquer it. See it for what it really is and you shall transform it into or even greater blessing.

See yourself. Know who and what you are, and know it absolutely: a child of G-d granted the power to be His partner in creation and in perfect in His world. All hindrance and limitation, all failure, is only the failure to see your true potential. See yourself, and there is nothing you cannot achieve. Look at yourself in the mirror and start to see the soul that you are, see the soul within the person you are facing.

See today. Do not merely "hear" goodness and G-dliness as an abstract concept; see it in the here and now, see its immediacy and its reliability. See it coming to light today. Walk down the street and notice both human goodness and also G-d' light up the world.

A Noahide who has sinned against G-d or his fellow man must repent and be sorry for what he has done. He must promise to himself that he will not commit this sin again. He will make a personal prayer to G-d, requesting mercy. If he has hurt a fellow person, he must request that person's forgiveness. If he has done damage to that person's property or body, he must compensate him. If he has done damage to himself, to his health or property or his family, he must make amends.

HERE ARE SOME POINTS TO PONDER

Why and how do we pray to G-d?

What is our relationship with G-d?

What is the connection between the body and soul?

Blessing and curse – good and evil – light and darkness.

CHAPTER - LAW 3

RESPECT FOR HUMAN LIFE - DO NOT MURDER

This principle teaches that human life is sacred. One must never do anything that would result in the death of a fellow human being; one must not derive any profit from the death of an innocent human being. This principle also considers abortion as well as euthanasia to be equivalent to murder. It is permissible to kill a murderer.

It is also permissible to kill in self-defense. One may also kill, if it is absolutely necessary to save an innocent person's life. This principle forbids suicide. You may not do anything that may endanger your own life. You must not do anything that endangers the lives of others. If you have a business, you must make sure that it does not endanger the safety of others.

G-D IS HOLY-LIFE IS HOLY

The Torah is primarily concerned with life on this world. The soul exists before its descent to earth and returns to the heavenly realm in the afterlife. It is a "descent for the purpose of ascent", the ascent being the fulfillment of the ultimate purpose in creation, the creation of a dwelling for G–d in this world.

King Solomon describes the soul as "the candle of G–d". For what purpose does G–d need a candle? Is there any place where it is dark before Him? The candle is needed for this world within which G–d has clothed His majesty. The soul illuminates the body and the world, enabling it to recognize the Creator, through fulfillment of the Torah and mitzvah in daily life.

A SPECIFIC PURPOSE

In addition, every soul has a specific purpose besides the general purpose of making a dwelling place for G–d in this world. The Baal Shem Tov said that a soul, in addition to keeping the Torah and mitzvoth, may descend to this world and live for 70 or 80 years just to do a favor for another in the physical or the spiritual sense. How does one know one's own specific purpose? How does one know, which favor is the purpose of one's soul's descent? The answer is that everything happens by Divine Providence and, if a person is presented with a certain opportunity, this is certainly sent from Above and should be treated as if it is the purpose of one's soul's descent.

Our Torah stated, "Everything is in the hands of Heaven, except the fear of Heaven." This means that whatever happens to a person is from Heaven. The particular time and place a person lives and his station in life, whether rich or poor etc., is decided from Heaven. A person's only contribution is "the fear of Heaven" – his reaction in any given situation. We are all presented with unique opportunities and challenges and it is our task in life to utilize them for the Divine purpose.

THE SOUL'S DESCENT

Our Sages stated further, the essential nature of the soul, its holiness and purity, and how it is completely divorced from anything material and physical; the soul itself, by its very nature, is not subject to any material desires or temptations, which arise only from the physical body and the animal soul".

Nevertheless, it was the Creator's Will that the soul – which is in the image of the Divine, should descend into the coarse, physical world and be confined within, and united with, a physical body for scores of years in a state which is diametrically opposed to its spiritual nature. All this for the purpose of a Divine mission which the soul has to perform to purify and elevate the physical body and its related physical environment, making this world an abode for the Divine Presence. This can be done only through a life of Torah and mitzvah's When the soul fulfils this mission all the transient pain and suffering connected with the soul's descent and life on this earth is not only justified, but infinitely outweighed, by the great reward and everlasting bliss which the soul enjoys thereafter.

A WASTED OPPORTUNITY

From the above one can easily appreciate the extent of the tragedy of disregarding the soul's mission on earth. For, in doing so, one causes the soul to descend to this world virtually in vain, for one has not achieved one's purpose. Even where there are brief moments of religious activity in the study of Torah and the practice of the commandments, it is sad to contemplate how often such activity is tainted by a lack of real enthusiasm and inner joy, without recognition that these are the activities which justify existence.

Apart from missing the vital point through failure to take advantage of the opportunity to fulfill G–d's will, thus forfeiting the eternal benefits to be derived from this the physical existence of ours, it is contrary to sound reason to choose that aspect of life which accentuates the enslavement and degradation of the soul, while rejecting the good that is within it namely, the great elevation, that is to come from the soul's descent.

The proper thing to do is to make the most of the soul's sojourn on earth, and a life which is permeated by the Torah and mitzvoth makes this possible. It is also abundantly clear, that since G–d, who is the essence of goodness, compels the soul to descend from its sublime heights to the lowest depths for the purpose of the study of the Torah and the fulfillment of the mitzvoth, it must mean that the value of Torah and mitzvoth is very great.

Furthermore, the descent of the soul for the purpose of being elevated shows that there is no other way to obtain this objective, except through the soul's descent to live on this earth. If there were an easier way, G–d would not compel the soul to descend to this nether world. For only here, in what the Kabbalists call the lowest world, can the soul attain its highest ascent, higher even than the angels, and, as our Sages say, "The righteous are superior to the (foremost) angels."

mankind -- "revolutionary" in the sense that it flies in the face of everything everyone previously believed (as indeed in the face of common sense), and "revolutionary" in the way it has transformed the face of civilized society.

Placing an infinite value on every human life means an utter rejection of any "scale" by which to qualify the worth of human life. A retarded baby's life has the same value as that of the wisest person on earth. An 80-year-old "vegetable" cannot be sacrificed to save the life of a 20-year-old genius.

Torah goes so far as to rule that an entire city cannot be saved by giving up a single individual for death. Because each and every life is of Divine - and therefore infinite -significance. Ten thousand infinities aren't any "more" than one infinity. An example euthanasia, abortion of deformed babies are forbidden, because life is a gift by G-d and in spite the fact we may not see it in a reveled manor.

In light of the above, it is surprising to find the following law in the Torah (derived from Deuteronomy 22:26): Habah l'hargecha hashken l'hargo -- "If someone is coming to kill you, rise against him and kill him first." (This law applies equally to someone coming to kill someone else -- you're obligated to kill the murderer in order to save his intended victim).

This law seems to contradict the principle of life's infinite value. If no life can be deemed less valuable that any other, what makes the victim's life more valuable than the murderer's life? Furthermore, this rule applies to anyone who is "coming to kill you" -- he hasn't even done anything yet! Maybe he won't succeed? Maybe he'll change his mind? Nor does the law say anything about trying to run away. It says: If someone is coming to kill you, rise against him and kill him first.

The same Torah that tells us that G-d placed a spark of Himself in every human being, thereby bestowing upon his or her physical existence a G-dly, infinite worth -- that same Torah also tells us that G-d has granted free choice to every person. Including the choice -- and the power -- to corrupt his or her G-d-given vitality and turn it against itself, using it to destroy life. A person can choose to turn himself into a murderer -- someone who is prepared to destroy life in order to achieve his aims- in which case he is no longer a life, but an anti-life.

To kill an anti-life is not a life-destroying act, it is a life-preserving act. It is not a violation of the commandment "Do not kill", but its affirmation. Without the law, "If someone is coming to kill you, rise against him and kill him first," the principle of life's infinite value is nothing more than an empty slogan, a mere idea. Judaism is not an idea. It is a way of life -- G-d's ideas made real.

HERE ARE SOME POINTS TO PONDER

What is our mission in this world?

Why is abortion forbidden?

Why is suicide forbidden?

Can we take a life when one asks? Euthanasia?

When must we kill a person?

CHAPTER - LAW 4

RESPECT FOR THE FAMILY - DO NOT COMMIT ADULTERY

The Torah acknowledges that a good sexual relationship between a husband and wife strengthens their marriage and love. It is accepted that a husband and wife should love each other and that their love should be passionate. The purpose of sex in a marriage is to perpetuate the human race and to create a close and permanent bond between the spouses and it is the marriage's foundation. It is a fundamental human need to experience love through physical closeness with a permanent mate in a secure long term relationship between spouses. The Torah forbids, i.e. Divinely defines as immoral, having sexual acts with a married person, committing homosexuality, incest, and bestiality.

"G-d blessed Noah and his children. He said to them, 'Be fruitful and multiply and fill the earth." (Genesis 9:1)

WHAT IS MARRIAGE?

The Torah teaches us, that marriage is not merely a union between two totally independent individuals. Marriage is the reunion between two halves of the same unit. A couple shares the same soul, which, upon birth, divides itself into two incomplete halves. Upon marriage, they reunite and become, once again, complete. What we are dealing with here is not only a union on the physical, emotional and/or intellectual level. What we are dealing with here is a union on the deepest, most essential level of self. There are souls that are compatible for marriage and there are souls that are not. Besides the case of mixed marriages, the Bible enumerates a list of invalid 'marriages', for example the 'marriage' between a biological brother and sister or between a man and a woman that is married to another man, in other words, incest or adultery. The Bible is not only talking here about prohibitions, but facts. In the aforementioned examples, there can never be any spiritual marriage, even though it might physically be possible to cohabitate and procreate for such individuals.

WHAT IS WRONG WITH INTERMARRIAGE?

We live today in a multi-cultural and multi-religious society. We mix freely with, and respect, people of all faiths. Many Jews today grow up fully assimilated and comfortable in a secular society and environment. Why is it such a tragedy if a Jewish man finds a non Jewish woman (or vice versa), with whom he feels totally compatible and decides to marry her? He claims that she is a genuinely lovely person with a fine character – often much nicer than any Jewish woman he has met. She is at home with his Jewish background and culture and they both share the same values, hobbies and pursuits. A perfect match, yet not made in Heaven. Why not?

The decision to marry out is perhaps the most telling moment, when a person must consider what the Torah or Bible actually states. There is a difference between a Jew and a non-Jew, in that each one has a different mission from G-d.

And now, at the time of marriage, a Divine institution in the G-dly tradition, a person wishes to change what the Creator set out in the Torah, Bible. We need accept the Divine law, which assigns to each and everyone of us as a unique task, to the non Jew and Jew alike, in making this world a dwelling place where the light of G-ds shines, as its states "and G-d will be king on all nations of the world". One task is not better then the other and both are vital and important and compliment one another.

Based on the above, we have a very simple explanation for our Jewish friend as to why we cannot consider him or her as potential marriage partners. It is simply due to the Biblical concept of marriage, we should respect everyone's unique quality and personality, however not as husband and wife.

IS CONVERSION AN OPTION FOR THE NON JEWISH?

Conversion into Judaism is serious business. Ask yourself this question: Is the conversion being carried out from a true desire to become Jewish, independent of any impending partnership, or is it a token conversion, done to please some parent or other relative? A serious conversion can take years and involves serious changes in lifestyle and conduct.

To undergo a "cosmetic" or "plastic" conversion is, obviously, not a acceptable solution to a seriously minded person, and even more abhorrent to an honest person. A true conversion has to be such as to transform a non-Jew into a Jew, with a new Jewish Neshamah, soul, like a newborn child of Jewish parents. Such a conversion is one that is carried out in strict accordance with Halachah, Jewish law; anything less is only a sham and a mockery.

The Halachah, Jewish law, is very clear in its insistence that the would-be convert honestly and wholeheartedly accepts all the mitzvoth, commandments without exception. Accepting all but one mitzvah automatically invalidates the conversion and the non-Jew remains a non-Jew exactly as before. Of course, it is possible to mislead a rabbi or a Rabbinic Court by declaring one's readiness to accept all the mitzvoth without really intending to, but one cannot mislead the Creator, who is the One who imbues the convert to Judaism with the Neshamah, soul.

There is the well known popular argument that it is unfair to demand more of a would-be convert, in terms of adherence to the mitzvoth, than that which many born Jews observe in practice. This contention is inadmissible since the complete commitment to Halachah is a requirement and stipulation of Jewish Law to which the would-be convert must unequivocally commit himself.

A word of caution: within the Jewish community today some would contend that one may convert in either an Orthodox or "Progressive" establishment. It should be clear from the start that an Orthodox conversion is accepted in all Jewish circles, whereas the Orthodox do not accept a Progressive conversion. To convert in a "Progressive" establishment is hazardous in itself; for one's Jewish identity is then not universally recognized.

The Noahide laws are a way that all non-Jews fulfill their divine mission and receive reward in the world to come just like any Jew that keeps the 613 commandments, we all are created by G-d in his Image, we all do not look or think the same... every human being that keeps the Torah's laws will have a share in the world to come.

HERE ARE SOME POINT TO PONDER

What is marriage? Why is same sex forbidden?

Why is marriage between Jews and Non -Jews not an option?

Why is conversion for the sake of marriage not an option?

Purpose of Sexual Relationship in Marriage?

CHAPTER - LAW 5

RESPECT FOR THE RIGHTS AND PROPERTY OF OTHERS - DO NOT STEAL

Honesty is called the principle of dominion; this teaches that G-d grants the right of property to each person. The person has control over the property that he holds for G-d. To steal the property of another is a perversion of this principle. That is why it is also called the principle of honesty. This principle teaches you that you must never steal anything from another; you must never deceive another person, or take anything dishonestly.

EVERYTHING IS G-DS

Chassidim like to tell the story about a certain individual who was flippant with his financial obligations. It reached the point that his debtors felt they had no recourse but to inform their Rebbe of the situation. The Chassidic sage summoned the man and asked him: "Is it true what they tell me -- that you borrow money and don't repay, that you buy on credit and then evade payment?"

"But Rebbe!" exclaimed the Chassid. "Haven't you taught us that the world is nothing, material cares are nothing, and money is nothing? Why are they making a fuss about a few rubles? It's all nothing!"

"In that case," said the Rebbe, "how about if we take this 'nothing' "and here the Rebbe pointed to the body of

41

the spiritual fellow -- "and we stretch it out upon this 'nothing' (the table), and with this 'nothing' (his belt) administer a dozen lashes to the first 'nothing'?"

Behind this humorous story lies a serious question. If, as the Psalmist proclaims, "The world, and all it contains, is G-d's", is there, in fact, such a thing as "theft"? Can something that does not, in truth, belong to you, be taken from you?

Of course, G-d said "You shall not steal." Those are the rules of the game. But maybe that's what it is -- a game. G-d is saying: "Let's make believe that this house belongs to Tom. And let's make believe that this car belongs to Harry. Now, Harry, you mustn't burn down 'Tom's house'. And Tom, you're not allowed to use 'Harry's car' without his permission." Is that what it amounts to?

According to the Torah of the 10 Commandment the Third Commandment, "You shall not take G-d's name in vain", and the Eighth Commandment, "You shall not steal", are one and the same. Indeed, the Torah (in Leviticus 5:20) refers to financial fraud as "a betrayal of G-d". "Because" explains the great Talmudic sage Rabbi Akiva, "in defrauding his fellow, he is defrauding the Third Party to their dealings." On the face of it, this can be understood along the lines of our "rules of the game" thesis. The problem with stealing is not that a certain person's "ownership" has been violated (since everything belongs to G-d anyway), but that the Divine command "You shall not steal" has been transgressed.

However if that were the case, asks the Lubavitcher Rebbe, why does Rabbi Akiva describe G-d as "the Third

Party to their dealings"? Isn't He the only party? Aren't we saying that it's G-d's car that's been stolen, and the fact that He chose to register it in Harry's name is basically irrelevant?

But Rabbi Akiva is being consistent. Remember the verse "The world, and all it contains, is G-d's"? Rabbi Akiva, quoting this verse in the Talmud, interprets it to be saying, "He acquired, and bequeathed, and rules His world." What does this mean? Isn't it G-d's world because He created it? And if He "bequeathed" it, than it's not His anymore!

What Rabbi Akiva is saying, explains the Rebbe, is this: Obviously, it's His because He created it. But then He desired to make it His in a deeper and more meaningful way -- by bequeathing it to man.

To own a world because you made it is basically meaningless. In human terms, that's like dreaming up a life and trying to derive satisfaction from your own fantasy. For something to be real for us, it has to have existence outside of ourselves. To derive pleasure from something, we have to share its existence with others.

G-d desired to derive pleasure from His world, viz. to have abode in this world. That's why He gave it to us, and asked us to share it with Him.

That's why He said: "Tom, this is your house. I mean it -- it is really and truly *yours*. Now this is what I would like you to do with it. I want you to put charity box in your kitchen. I want it to be a place that shelters a moral family life, a place in which hospitality is extended to the needy, a place where My Torah, the Bible is studied. "Of course, I could just put you in this house and tell you to do all this, without really giving it to you. But then you'd be doing all these things mechanically, like a robot. Deep down, you would sense that it's not really your home, that the things you're doing are not really your achievement. And then it wouldn't ever be truly My home, either. It would just be something I made up.

"That's why I gave it to you. You sense it to be yours because it really is. You experience what you make of it to be your own achievement, because it really is. And when you choose, with the free will that I have granted you, to invite Me into your home and make Me at home in it, it will become truly mine, too, in the manner that I desire it to be mine.

"And please, don't steal Harry's car. Because I have a stake in every financial transaction that occurs between the two of you. When you deprive Harry of the ownership that I have given him over his piece of My world, you are depriving Me as well. You are making My ownership of My world all but meaningless."

THE FIRST COMMENTARY

The Torah begins and Rashi asks a question about the first verse of the first chapter of the first book of the Torah, "In the beginning G-d created Heaven and earth." Rashi's question is, why does the Torah begin with a description of creation rather than with commandments? Since the Torah is basically a book of commandments and a guide as to how we should behave in our daily life, the Torah should get right down to instructing us on our behavior. And yet it begins with a lengthy description of

44

creation and the history of what happened from creation until the giving of the Torah. Rashi answers that this was done because there would come a time when the nations would accuse the Jews of being thieves and imperialists. They would say, "You stole the land from the nations!" Therefore, the Torah begins with the story of creation

We will say: "G-d created Heaven and earth. Earth belongs to G-d. He gave The Holy Land to the Canaanites for a while, and then he took it from them and gave it to us." So our answer is that we can't "steal" the land because it belongs to G-d, and G-d gives it to whomever he wants. He wants the Holy Land of Israel to be under full ownership and control of His people Israel to live in it according to His Torah, including treating the non-Jewish residents and visitors according to His code of behavior, of kindness, fairness and justice.

THE HOLY LAND OF ISRAEL

The Rebbe points out that this Rashi, which is basically a quote from the Talmud, doesn't say "the Land of Israel." It doesn't say we will be accused of stealing "the Land of Israel" -- it says that we will be accused of stealing the land of the nations. What is "the land of the nations"?

All lands can be conquered, however since G-d gave the Land of Israel to the children of Israel, no other nation can own it.

Thus, G-d starts the Torah with "in the beginning G-d created the heavens and the earth

The Land of Israel is central in Judaism and belongs to every Jewish person regardless if they live in Israel, and non-Jewish people are welcome as long as they keeps the Laws of Noah.

HERE ARE SOME POINTS TO PONDER

Why is stealing not permitted?

The land of Israel was given by G-d to the Jewish people. And the Bible, Torah begins Genesis…

Everything comes from G-d.

The purpose of creation is that we elevate and make a dwelling place for G-d

The world is fundamentality good we should cherish and appreciate it

Why does the Land of Israel belong to the Jewish people?

CHAPTER - LAW 6

CREATING LAW AND ORDER - ESTABLISH LAWS AND COURTS OF JUSTICE

Since G-d is just, so must you be just. Justice is the foundation of civilization. When justice ceases to exist, civilization crumbles, when criminals are not punished, they gain power and take over, and one should therefore do everything in their power to see that criminals are punished. This is especially true of criminals who violate the Torah's principles as well as the laws of the land. Also one should not benefit from any crime or criminal action.

For example the first Jew, Abraham, distinguished himself from those he lived amongst by demanding, "Will the Judge of all the earth then not do justice?" The idea that there is a Judge and there is justice, reward and punishment, that it is up to us to fulfill G-d's will, all this, Maimonides says, is the very basis of Torah and its commandments. And so is G-d's omnipotence. By exploring these two concepts and the resolution our tradition has provided, we are exploring the very core of Judaism.

IS THE WORLD NECESSARY?

The ancient Greeks thought so--and this perspective has persisted throughout philosophy to this day: The world is here because it must be here.

Jews, however, disagree. "You are the beginning and You are the end and who can tell You what to do?" Creation is a deliberate act. It happens only, because He chose it should happen. Even after a world exists, it remains "unnecessary".

In short, Torah grants G-d free choice.

This idea is difficult for the rational mind, because it is impossible to create a model for it. True randomness and spontaneity is entirely out of the range of mathematics. Even today's chaos theories are based on procedural models. We can't create a system that will choose randomly with no explanation for why it has chosen either way--a system of effect without cause. Typical of human intuition, we imagine that since there is no mathematical model for something, G-d is not allowed to do it.

Let's return to this idea that the cosmos enters into being simply out of G-d willing it so. Let's explore a simple question: Does G-d *have to* make a world? In other words, does the supposition that there is an Infinite Essential Being, who is capable of creating a world determine, that therefore a world *must* come into being? Or, as a philosopher would put it…

Today's concept of science, however, has brought us to think in larger terms, surrendering to the idea that there are things that do not fit--and do not have to fit--into our neat little models (such as the essential reality). It is this surrender that has allowed us to come up with relativity and quantum mechanics. It also makes it easier for us to conceive of this idea of choice, which is so fundamental to Jewish thought.

TO BE AND NOT TO BE

G-d's omnipotence, then, allows Him to choose to create a world or to not create a world. As the Lubavitcher Rebbe interprets the words of Maimonides, G-d has both the power of being and of not being. He chooses being, so a world exists. At the same time He chooses not being--as we will explain. Let's look at a small analogy that will serve as something of a handle to grasp a very abstract idea.

All the analogies we need are provided within the human psyche, "for in the image of G-d, He created the human being." The balanced human adult is the closest model of the cosmic process we can get.

One token quality of an adult human being is the ability to hold back. A child feels compelled to speak and do whatever arises in his mind. For an eloquent demonstration, ask a child to help another child with homework--it's next to impossible for them to help without giving the answers away. True, many adults have the same problem, but a mature mind is able to provide just what is necessary and then stand by while the student explores and discovers all on his/her own. At times the student may fail, or go off on dead-end tangents. A true adult is able to sit and watch, perhaps even assist the student to explore false options, and provide only what is necessary to ensure an eventual successful resolution.

Through silence, the adult communicates more than through overt instruction. Instruction provides information. Unspoken guidance provides the student with his/her own mind. A careful balance of the two is the mark of an excellent teacher.

The act of creation, and all those things that occur instantaneously "because He so wills it" are somewhat analogous to overt instruction. He wants it, He says it, and it is. All this extends from His "power of being".

But there are also things that He wills, yet withholds. That doesn't mean He doesn't tell us about them. In some cases He may, in some not--at least, not overtly. But He, so to speak, restrains His words from their fruition, allowing us to achieve that result. He lets us know that we should care for each other, but allows us to do the opposite--and experience the consequences. He lets us know He wants a world where Charity below is in concordance with Charity from above--but leaves the fulfillment of His desire up to us. In very many cases, He leaves it up to us to determine what it is that He wants-- instructing us only that we must rely on those who are accepted sages of His Torah.

In the Torah, G-d gives us a taste of His "power of not being"--and provides us something of Himself that His act of creation does not, more accurately, Torah contains a balance of the two powers of being and not being, revealing and withholding, instructing and allowing failure--and it is through this balance that we are able to touch the Essence from whence all opposites extend, as well as our own essential selves. Once again, the ever-repeating epithet of Torah, *Havaye hu HaElokim*--"The

G-d of revelation is the same G-d as the G-d of concealment". And therefore, "There is nothing else but He."

This is also the meaning of the statement, "The Torah preceded the world": Even after creation of a world according to the blueprint of Torah, the Divine will contained in Torah remains beyond it. Our mission is to funnel that higher plane into our reality. We do that by exercising our own free choice, which is, in fact, a reflection of His, G-ds free choice which we have just described.

HERE ARE SOME POINT TO PONDER

Why do we need laws? They are man made?

The Torah, bible is the first book of law that's fair and timeless…

Torah is Divine and is the blueprint of creation.

What is the concept of free choice?

The Torah justice is concerted with absolute truth.

One the witness a crime can not be a judge.

RESPECT FOR ALL CREATURES - DO NOT BE CRUEL TO ANIMALS

The principle of kindness, must be extended to every human being and every living creature. For example the Jewish commandment that one must feed one's animals before one sits down to eat is directly related to this principle. It is permissible to eat meat, but first the animal must be slaughtered or killed in the manner least painful to the animal. When you show kindness to G-d's creatures, G-d will show kindness to you.

The consumption of the limb of a living animal, for example, eating a live lobster is forbidden and is associated with cruelty to animals. The universal spiritual code is known as the "Seven Noahide laws". The reason for this name is because, although six of the laws were commanded to the first person, Adam, the seven laws were completed with Noah, to whom the seventh commandment was given. Only after the flood, it was permitted to humanity to slaughter meat for consumption, and with this came the law prohibiting one to eat the limb of a living animal.

If Judaism requires us to be kind to animals, shouldn't we be commanded to be vegetarians? I have the utmost respect for anyone who chooses not to eat meat out of concern for animal welfare. And there have been some who have suggested that this is in keeping with Judaism's ideals, although all agree that Judaism allows eating meat.

However there is another way of looking at it, a more spiritual angle, which indicates that eating meat is not just an accommodation to human desire, but has a holy purpose.

The Talmud teaches that the reason Adam and Eve were created after all other creatures was to teach them a dual lesson: humans can be either the pinnacle of creation, or its lowest life-form. If they act appropriately, then everything was created just to serve them; but if they degrade themselves, then they should remember that "even a flea preceded you."

FREE WILL

The human being is the only creature with free will. This means we can either work on ourselves and become better than our nature, or abuse our gifts and become worse. Only a human can be generous, kind, selfless and act higher than his or her instincts; and only a human can be cruel, destructive and murderous. Although sometimes animals do what seem like acts of kindness or destruction, they are invariably just following their instinct for survival -- there is no altruism or malice in their actions.

When we use our freedom to act in a kind, holy and selfless way, we are the highest life form, and the rest of creation is there for us. Then, by eating other creatures we are in fact elevating them to places where they couldn't go by themselves.

For example, if I eat a tomato, and then expend the energy that that tomato gave me in performing an act of kindness, the tomato has become a partner in my action, thus making the world a better place -- something a tomato can't do on its own.

On the other hand, if I use my energy only to further selfish goals, or to oppress or inflict harm, then what right do I have to eat a tomato? The tomato never hurt anybody, and by eating it and causing harm I am corrupting an innocent tomato!

This is why Judaism doesn't see eating animals as necessarily being cruel. In fact, it could even be cruel not to eat animals, because you are robbing them of a chance to serve a higher purpose (unless of course it is for health reasons). However if you yourself are not living a life of purpose, then it is just as cruel to eat a tomato as a chicken! Since you are debasing all these life forms.

COMPASSION NOT UNDERSTANDING

The Talmud states: Rabbi Yehuda HaNassi was a perfect tzaddik, a righteous person even though he suffered great pain. How did it begin? Through a deed of his. He was walking through the marketplace when a calf being led to the slaughter ran to him and hid under his cloak. He told the sheep, "Go. For this you were created." That is when his suffering began.

And it ended through another deed. His maid was sweeping the floor and found the young of a weasel nested beneath the boards. She began to sweep them away, when he stopped her. "It is written," he said, "that

His compassion is upon all of His works." That is when his suffering ceased.

We are meant to not understand, because not understanding is what allows us to have compassion.

Rabbi Israel Baal Shem Tov (1698-1760), in the years that he was a hidden mystic, would make his livelihood slaughtering chickens and beef for Jewish communities before a festival. When he left this occupation, a new slaughterer took his place. One day, the gentile helper of one of the Jewish villagers brought a chicken to the new slaughterer. As the new man began to sharpen his knife, the gentile watched and began to laugh. "You wet your knife with water before you sharpen it!" the gentile exclaimed, "And then you just start to cut?"

"And how else?" the slaughterer asked. "Yisroelik -the Baal Shem Tov would cry until he had tears enough to wet the knife. Then he would cry as he sharpened the knife. Only then would he cut!" replied the gentile.

The Torah commands us not to cause unnecessary pain to any living being. No distinction is made whether that living being is a cow or a lizard or a fly. The Rebbe Rabbi Sholom Dovber of Lubavitch once scolded his son, the Rebbe Rayatz, for tearing up a leaf of a tree, saying, "What makes you think that the 'I' of the leaf is the lesser than your own 'I'?"

Even when it is deemed necessary to consume the life of another, there are rules. An empty-minded person, the sages taught, has no right to eat meat. They also said to never eat meat out of hunger-first satisfy the hunger with bread. A person who eats meat solely for his palate and for his stomach degrades both himself and the animal. However if it is "mindful eating"- eating for the sake of harnessing that animal's energies to do good; eating that lifts the animal into a new realm of being; eating to give at least as much to the animal as it gives to us - then it becomes a way of connecting with the Divine and elevating our universe.

As for the angels and their part in the deal, "Once the Temple was destroyed," the Talmud tells, "the table of every man atones for him."Your table is an altar. The angels are invited. Eat with humility and with compassion and with mindfulness. Do your part in the Divine cycle of life.

HERE ARE SOME POINT TO PONDER

What is the relationship between food and a person's spiritual life?

Being kind and feeding your animal before you eat... (Or one's children...)

Having empathy for others and caring after your environment

What is free will?

CHAPTER - 8

CHARITY, GIVING TO RECEIVE

T his principle is a basic feature of humanity. For the human being is, to use the biblical phrase, "created in the Divine Image"; thus the giving of charity, which brings sustenance to a needy individual, is a life-sustaining act--one that effectively allows us to imitate G-d, "Who gives life to all living creatures." therefore G-d has provided us an opportunity for the noblest of life's endeavors--to "walk in His ways." The Hebrew word Tzedakah, commonly translated as "charity," literally means "justice" or "righteousness." "Charity" connotes a generosity of spirit--giving of the rich to the poor. "Tzedakah," on the other hand, implies that one is fulfilling his or her obligation in doing what is just and right. One is giving not of one's own, but of that which has been entrusted by G-d to him or her, for the purpose of giving to others what they need.

RICH AND POOR

In our world, so blatantly and at times brutally dichotomized by prosperity and poverty, there exist two general perspectives on wealth and property:

1) That these are the rightful possession of those who earned or inherited them. If they choose to share even a small a part of their possessions with others, this is a noble act, worthy of praise and acclaim.

2) That the unequal distribution of the earth's resources among its inhabitants is a travesty. Owning more than one's share is an injustice, even a crime. Giving to the needy is not a "good deed" but the rectification of a wrong.

Jewish belief rejects both these views. According to Torah law, giving to the needy is both a mitzvah -- a commandment and a good deed. This means that, on the one hand, it is not an arbitrary act, but a duty and an obligation. On the other hand, it is a good deed -- a credit to the one who recognizes his duty and carries out his obligation. The Torah believes that material wealth is not a crime, but a blessing from G-d. One who has so been blessed should regard himself as G-d's "banker" -- one who is privileged to have been entrusted by the Creator with the role of dispensing the resources of His creation to others.

G-d could have allotted equal portions of His world to all its inhabitants. But then the world would have been nothing more than a showpiece of G-d's creative powers, predictable as a computer game and static as a museum display. G-d wanted a dynamic world -- a world in which man, too, is a creator and provider. A world in which the controls have, to a certain extent, been handed over to beings who have the power to choose between fulfilling or reneging on their role.

Therefore Jewish law requires every individual to give charity, even one who is himself sustained by the charity of others. If the purpose of charity were merely to rectify the unequal distribution of wealth between rich and poor, this law would make no sense, Charity, however, is much more than that: it is the opportunity granted to every person to become a "partner with G-d in creation." Giving charity is, above all, a humbling experience. Before us stands a human being less fortunate than ourselves. We know that G-d could have just as easily provided him with everything he requires, instead of sending him to us for his needs. Here is a person who is suffering poverty in order to provide us with the opportunity to do a G-dly deed!

By the same token, if Divine providence places us on the receiving end of a charitable act, we need not be demoralized by the experience. For we know that G-d could have just as easily provided us with all that we need Himself, and that our need for human aid is merely in order to grant another person the ability to do a G-dly deed. Our "benefactor" is giving us money or some other resource; we are giving him something far greater the opportunity to become a partner with G-d in creation.

In the words of our sages: "More than the rich man does for the pauper, the pauper does for the rich man."

HOW TO GIVE

Giving is the easy part. It's the receiving part that's so difficult. How many people do you know who have mastered the art of graciously receiving a gift or a compliment? Why, many of us find it hard to bring ourselves to ask for directions! We all want to be independent.

There is a reason, why this is so. Man, we are told, was created in the image of his Creator. Giving comes naturally to the source of all. But how can one who lacks for nothing receive? Only by an act of self-contraction, by the great mystery of a Divine will that proclaims: "I desire thus from you." Contrary to the modern belief that is person is the independent master of his own fate and also his own financial success Torah posits that G-d's blessing is critical both for preserving all the good we have, including our relationships, and also increasing our station in life. The more we align our Divine will the more we see blessings.

Created in the Divine Image, man is a natural giver. But it requires a supreme effort on our part in order to genuinely receive, to hollow the self into a receptive vessel for a bestowal of love.

An even greater challenge is the endeavor to be a true recipient in the very act of giving. To convey to the recipient of our gift--as G-d conveys to us--how deeply we desire to give, and how grateful we are for having been granted the opportunity to do so.

There was a Chassid who, whenever he was approached with the request for a donation for charity, would stick his hand into his pocket and take out a few coins. Then, with a hastily mumbled "just a minute...," he would again dig into his pocket and come up with another few coins.

Someone who noticed his custom once asked him: "Why do you always give in two installments? Could you not take out the full sum you want to give at once?"

"Every act of charity is a victory over our selfish nature," replied the Chassid. "I just can't resist the opportunity to score two victories for the price of one..."

CHARITY IS AFFORDABLE

Some people are scared to give charity because they worry their funds might be depleted. Nonsense, I say. The more you give, the more you get. Others argue that we must be cautious when distributing charity, to make sure the funds are allocated properly. However sometimes it is a life or death situation. For example one of the reasons we don't make a blessing on the mitzvah, commandment of giving charity, like on all other mitzvoth, is because if we pause even for a minute, the beggar might be gone.

Most importantly, charity is accomplished not only by distributing money, but in many other ways -- by giving advice, educating a fellow human being, visiting the sick, having guests for a meal, returning lost property. Sometimes even a simple smile can be a great act of giving.

There is a story about the Rebbe, Rabbi Shmuel of Lubavitch (1834-1882) and his wife, Rebbetzin Rivkah. Rabbi Shmuel would travel often, sometimes his wife would travel with him, and on several occasions his wife stayed home. Before departing, Rabbi Shmuel would give Rebbetzin Rivkah money for all the necessary living expenses, including large sums for distributing to charity. Being that Rebbetzin Rivkah was very generous, the charity allowance left by her husband would run out quickly, and she would pawn off her personal belongings and jewelry, to earn extra charity funds for the poor.

When the Rebbe, Rabbi Shmuel would come home he would immediately ask his wife Rivkah where she sold her belongings, and he would gladly redeem every last item.

We might not all be able to emulate this type of generosity. But surely we can afford a dollar a day, or a loaf of bread, or at least a smile and a word of encouragement, to our friends, our neighbors or a stranger in the dark.

The Lubavitcher Rebbe once suggested something beautiful and powerful: Every kitchen should have a charity box, so as to remind us before every meal that there are needy people who don't enjoy three meals a day, or even a kitchen. We ought to help them any way we can.

HERE ARE SOME POINT TO PONDER

Giving because you imitate G-d kindness.

Help is not just money.

How you give is important.

Honoring your parents, helping the sick.

Giving is not just money, a good word, and smile.

Giving charity is a humbling experience.

CHAPTER - 9

ACTS OF GOODNESS & KINDNESS

Many people feel that life in accordance with Torah and mitzvoth- commandments are restrictive, limiting the individual in personal creativity, particularly in the area of thinking and choosing for oneself. It is hard to reconcile such commitment with the idea of personal freedom. Furthermore, is it necessary to have the shackles of G-ds Torah to be a good person? There are thousands of people who are good, moral and decent human beings, however non-Noahides. They engage in acts of kindness both within the Jewish and non-Jewish communities. They lead active lives and many are role models in the worlds of science, art and commerce, however they do not keep the Noahide laws, in a sense of accepting the covenant with the Creator giving to them through Moses on Mount Sinai. What is wrong with being a good person but not a Noahide?

CAN ONE BE A GOOD PERSON WITHOUT BEING A NOAHIDE?

We all wish to live a good life. Most of us think that this means having the best of what life has to offer: a good and supportive family, good parents, a good spouse, good children and grandchildren. A good income and home. A good environment and community, good friends, and – most important – having a good time. A sum total of all good things equals a good life. A person starting out in life is faced with the puzzling question of how to create this good life.

Taking a look around us we see that life is far from perfect and full of pitfalls. In today's modern fast-moving world, more and more children are born into broken homes, more couples are splitting up and more people are suffering from depression and lack of self esteem. More people are discovering that material wealth does not ensure the road to happiness. More people are taking pills, drugs and tranquillizers. You have to be very lucky indeed to hit the jackpot and have all the factors in place to create the good life. In the end most of us settle for mediocrity, acknowledging that you can't have everything in life, a somewhat sobering but pragmatic conclusion. What is, therefore, the secret of the good life?

G–D IS GOOD

G–d, the Creator of man, who is also Creator and Master of the whole world, surely has the best qualifications that might be expected of any authority to know what is good for man and for the world in which he lives. G–d has not withheld this knowledge from us. G–d is good and it is the nature of good to be good. In His infinite kindness He has communicated to us, that if a person conducts his life in a certain way, he will have a healthy soul in a healthy body, and it will be good for him in this world and in the World to Come. It just makes plain common sense that in order to have a good life one should follow the directives of the Creator of man, even if there are aspects of those directives which superficially seem restrictive or difficult to accept.

An analogy may be drawn from a car. Before one steps into a car it is highly advisable to consult the manual in order to achieve the best performance levels from the car. Anyone who ignore the instructions could damage the car and, in some cases, the driver as well.

In truth there are many things in daily life which a person accepts and follows without question, even if he be a highly gifted intellectual with a searching bent of mind. For example, a person will board a plane without having first researched aerodynamics to verify that it is safe to fly in and that it will bring him to his destination at the scheduled time.

To take an example from the area of physical health: there are drugs which are known to be useful or harmful to one's health and a person would not go about trying to verify the utility or harmfulness of such a drug through personal experimentation. Even if a person had a very strong inclination to research and experiment, he would surely choose those areas which have not previously been researched.

This generally accepted attitude is quite understandable and logical. For, inasmuch as experts have amply researched these areas and have determined what is good and what is harmful for physical health, or have established the methods leading to further technological advancement, it would be a waste of time to repeat those experiments from the beginning. Furthermore, there is no assurance that some error may not be made leading to the wrong conclusions being drawn, possibly with disastrous effects.

What has been said above concerning physical health is also true in regard to spiritual health, and the means by which the soul can attain perfection and fulfillment. All the more so, since spiritual health is generally related to physical health, particularly insofar as a person is concerned.

TORAH IS TRUTH

It is quite certain that if a human being would live long enough, and would have the necessary capacities to make all sorts of experiments without distraction, interference or error, he would undoubtedly arrive at the very same conclusions which we already find in the Torah; namely, the need to observe the Noahide laws. The reason for this is that the Torah is the truth and is the ultimate good for a person.

But G–d, in His infinite goodness, wished to spare us all the trouble, as well as the possibility of error, and has already given us the results beforehand for the benefit both of those, who have the inclination and capacity to search, as well as for those who do not. G–d has definitely left areas where a person can carry on his own experiments in other areas which do not interfere with the rules laid down by Him.

Stated simply, the directives of the Torah are not a set of rules that have been given to impede or restrict the freedom of man. Rather, they are the pathway to a good life.

A fictional story is told of a bird during the days of creation. This particular bird was created without wings and when it looked around at other birds soaring in the heavens, it implored the Creator to allow it to fly. That night, whilst the bird was asleep, G–d affixed wings to its body. When the bird awoke and saw two new appendages to its body it said to G–d, "G–d, I asked you to make me fly, not to make me heavier." G–d replied, "little bird, just flap them and you will see that you will fly." The restrictions often seem like extra baggage but once we utilize them, they allow us to fly and soar into new heights.

The Torah places many restrictions on a person. The answer is that in every generation and age there is a form of bondage; an "Egypt". Some people are slaves to their jobs, others to the desires of their body. Some worship money, others power. Torah is the antidote that frees a person from his personal bondage. It maneuvers a person into the enviable position of being able to maximize the goodness of this world, as well as the next.

G–d is not an tyrant or ruthless dictator who insists on His subjects keeping a meaningless routine. G–d is benevolent and good and wishes to bestow good upon His creation. The greatest act of Divine benevolence, was to give us a living Torah – a pathway through life which leads us to the greatest good a human may achieve both for his body and soul. In short, if a person wants to have good relationships with his parents, spouse or children he should follow the directives of the Torah. If he wishes for Divine benevolence he must dispense charity to the needy. These are the pathways, not only to bliss in the

World to Come, but also to a meaningful and fulfilling life in this world.

In describing how a person must accept the commandments, the Rabbis often use the expression "acceptance of the yoke of mitzvoth", which may imply that the mitzvoth are somewhat of a burden. However, the true meaning of this expression is to be understood in the sense that human nature makes it necessary to act on imperatives. For human nature and the Yetzer Hara, evil inclination are such that an individual might easily succumb to temptation. Temptation is sweet at the beginning but bitter at the end and human nature may lead an individual to disregard the bitter consequences because of the initial gratification. We see, for example, that children and very often adults also, may be warned that over-indulgence in certain foods would be harmful to them and may even make them so ill that for a period of time they may not be able to eat anything at all, yet they nevertheless reject all restraint to gratify their immediate appetite. In a like manner G–d has given us the "yoke" of Torah and mitzvoth, telling us that whether one understands them or not, or whatever the temptation may be, one must carry out G–d's commandments unquestioningly.

THE DIVINE BRIDGE

There is a further point, and this is the most essential part of the concept of "yoke" of the Torah and mitzvoth. It is that although the Torah and mitzvoth have been given for the benefit of man, there is an infinitely greater quality with which G–d has endowed the Torah and mitzvoth. This is the quality of uniting man with G–d – that is, the created with the Creator – with whom he would otherwise have nothing in common. For, by giving man a set of mitzvoth, commandments to carry out in his daily life, G–d has made it possible for man thereby to attach himself to his Creator and transcend the limitations of time and space.

The Torah and mitzvoth constitute the bridge which spans the abyss separating the Creator from the created, enabling the human being to rise and attach himself to G–dliness. This bridge has been designed by G–d, for only He can span that abyss. It is quite impossible for a limited being to create his own bridge to the Infinite, for whatever bridge he may build, however spiritual it may be, it will still be limited according to the parameters of the created mind. This explains why a person cannot create his own path to G–d independent of Torah and mitzvoth. Torah is a revelation from Above, "And G–d came down on Mount Sinai". It is He who reached out to us and provided the path to Him.

Of course this relationship can only be attained, if the person observes the Torah and mitzvoth, not because of the reward contained therein, whether for the body or the soul, but purely because it is the will and command of G–d. It is for this reason that the text of the blessing which a person makes before fulfilling a mitzvah does not mention the utility of the mitzvah, rather the fact that G–d has sanctified us with His commandments and commanded us.

The very word "mitzvah" means both a commandment and a connection. The mitzvoth span the entire spectrum of human experience and give man the opportunity to be in sync with the Divine in both his spiritual and mundane affairs.

In fact, the essence of Judaism is the belief in a Creator, who brings the entire creation into existence from nothing every single second. His purpose is to create a physical world in which a person will create a fitting dwelling place for the Divine. This is achieved by connecting every aspect of the creation with the Creator. In short, a continuous performance of commandments.

ULTIMATE HAPPINESS

Even in man's most mundane activities he must connect with G–d. Before eating he must recite a blessing, realizing who is the Creator of the food. Whilst honoring parents he must realize that this commandment equal to honoring G–d.

The Torah teaches, "The reward for a mitzvah is a mitzvah." Some commentaries explain this in the literal sense that the reward for a mitzvah is the opportunity to perform another mitzvah. However, in the light of the above, one may explain that the reward of a mitzvah is the very connection that the person has with his Creator whilst he is doing the mitzvah.

This connection is life itself. In a Jewish context life may be defined as something eternal, whereas death is something that is interrupted. The Rabbis teach that the righteous, even in death, are alive. The pleasures of this world are momentary. They may last for a minute, an hour, a week, or even a few years but, after a while, are gone. Life – true life – is eternal. When engaging in mitzvah performance, a person is connecting with G–d, and therefore with eternity itself, and so is truly alive. That connection lasts forever and stands above time. The righteous are alive even after death because their entire focus in this world is their connection with G–d which continues even after death. And the Ben Noah also shares in this eternal existence.

This leads us to the true definition of happiness. Ultimate happiness may not be gauged by any amount of self-gratification, even of a spiritual nature. True happiness may be defined as the knowledge that one is doing the will of G–d at any given moment. Such happiness is constant and permanent. A person may serve G–d with joy even when going through difficult moments. That attachment is, in fact, the true goodness that a person may experience, for it is an experience of G–d Himself. In fact, the greatest good that G–d could possibly give us, is Himself.

To explain further: The world is a creation by G–d and, as such, can have no common denominator with its creator. This world consists of a variety of creatures which are generally classified into four "kingdoms": minerals, vegetation, animals and mankind. Taking the highest individual of the highest group of the four, i.e. the most intelligent of all men, there can be nothing in common between him – a created and limited being – and G–d – the Infinite Creator.

However, G–d gave us the possibility of approach and communion with Him by showing us the way that a finite created being can reach beyond his inherent limitations and commune with the Infinite. Obviously, only the Creator Himself knows the ways and means that lead to Him, and only the Creator Himself knows the capacity of His creatures in using such ways and means. Herein lies one of the most essential aspects of the Torah and mitzvoth. Although, to many, the Torah may be a means to gain reward and avoid punishment or just a guide to good living, being G–d given it has infinite aspects, and one of the most important is that it provides the means whereby we may reach a plane above and beyond our status as created beings. Clearly, this plane is far beyond the highest perfection which a man can obtain within his own created – and hence limited – sphere.

From this point of view it no longer appears strange that the Torah and mitzvoth find expression in such simple, material aspects as in, for example, the Noahide laws. For our intellect is also created and therefore limited within the boundaries of creation beyond which it has no access. Consequently, it cannot know the ways and means that lead beyond those bounds. The Torah, on the other hand, is the bond that unites the created with the Creator, as it is written, "And you that cleave to G–d, your G–d, are all living this day." To the Creator all created things, the most corporeal as well as the most spiritual, are equally removed. The question, "what relationship can a material object have with G–d?", has no more validity than if it referred to the most spiritual thing in its relationship to G–d.

The beauty of Torah and mitzvoth is that through simple everyday actions – well within the reach of normal individuals – every person can connect with the Divine and transform this world into an dwelling place for G–d. The Torah is not in heaven, rather, "it is exceedingly near to you, in your mouth and in your heart to do it."

Now let us return to the original question – can a person be a good without being observant? The answer is that even if a person lives what he personally considers to be a good and moral life and engages in acts of kindness etc., although he is partially fulfilled through the mitzvoth he is doing (and living a good and moral life is truly desirable in the eyes of G–d), he is nonetheless denying himself the maximum and optimum goodness available and so missing out on a very precious opportunity, by not utilizing his potential for a deeply fulfilling relationship with the Creator.

THE TRUE MEANING OF GOOD

In truth, without the Torah, which illuminates and gives directives to our rather complicated and rushed lives, we could possibly make a mistake as to what good means. Self-evident moral precepts, if left to human judgment without the binding force of Divine direction and sanction, can out of self-love be distorted so as to turn vice into virtue. Interpreting the moral precepts of "Thou shalt not kill ... Thou shalt not steal" from the viewpoint of selfish gain, many a nation, as well as many an individual, have "legalized" their abhorrent ends, not to mention justifying the means to those ends.

If in a previous generation there were people who doubted the need of Divine authority for common morality and ethics in the belief that human reason is sufficient, our present generation has unfortunately, in a most devastating and tragic way refuted this mistaken notion. For it is precisely the nation which excelled in the exact sciences, humanities and even in philosophy and ethics, that turned out to be the most depraved nation of the world, making an ideal of robbery and murder. Anyone who knows how insignificant was the minority of Germans who opposed the Hitler regime realizes that the German cult was not something which was practiced by a few individuals but it had embraced the vast majority of that nation, which considered itself the "super-race".

From this blatant historic example it is obvious that moral standards cannot be determined by individuals alone, for their human partiality will color their values. Rather, humankind should rely on a more absolute standard of goodness and morality which is set out by G–d in the values of the Torah. And it is no coincidence at all the defeated German gave itself in 1948 a constitution which mentions G-d in the very first line of the new constitution protecting human rights based on the Divine Image.

One of the basic messages of the Ten Commandments is contained in their opening words, "I am the L–rd your G–d" – the profound principle of monotheism which, in itself, was a tremendously revolutionary idea in those days of idolatry, dominated by the polytheistic culture of Egypt. This is detailed in the second commandment where all forms of idolatry are strictly prohibited. At the same time, the Ten Commandments conclude with such apparently simple and obvious injunctions as "Thou shalt not steal" etc.

The profundity of monotheism, with which the Ten Commandments begin, and the simplicity of the ethics and moral laws with which they conclude, point to two important lessons:

1. The true believer in G–d is not the one who holds abstract ideas, but the one whose knowledge of G–d leads him to the proper daily conduct even in ordinary and commonplace matters, in his dealings with his neighbors and respect for their property.

2. The ethical and moral laws, even those that are so obvious as "Thou shalt not murder" and "Thou shalt not steal", will have actual validity and be observed only if they are based on the first and second commandments; that is to say, based on Divine authority, the authority of the One and only G–d, and abandonment of all other objects of false worship, including in our day the human ego.

The Ten Commandments emphasize, and experience has fully and repeatedly borne out, that even the simplest precepts of morality and ethics must rest on the foundation of "I am G–d" and "Thou shalt have no other G–ds" and only then can their compliance be assured. Torah and mitzvoth alone provide the true content of Jewish law and are at the same time the fountains of life for each and every person.

A life of Torah and mitzvoth is the surest path to a good life. It is the very best thing for a human being and will bring him to the greatest fulfillment in this world.

The greatest good a person may experience is G–d Himself. This connection is achieved through Torah and mitzvoth. The Torah is compared to light, live with light

First it is necessary to start observing the mitzvoth and eventually we will almost certainly come to a better appreciation of their significance and truth. To approach this matter from the opposite direction; that is, to understand first and only then to do, is wrong on two scores. First, the loss involved in not performing mitzvoth cannot be retrieved.

Secondly, the very observance of the mitzvoth, which creates an immediate bond with G–d, develops additional powers, which help us to understand and appreciate them. Take, for instance, a person who is ill and for whom medicine has been prescribed by a specialist. Would it not be foolish to say that he should not take it until he knew how the medicine could restore him to good health? In the meantime, he would remain weak and ill and probably get even worse. It is senseless because the knowledge of how the medicine does its work is not necessary in order to benefit from it. Moreover, while taking it he will get a clearer head and better understanding to learn how the prescription helps him.

To expand on this theme, the world is a well co-ordinate system created by G–d in which there is nothing superfluous or lacking. There is one reservation, however: for reasons best known to the Creator He has given man free will, whereby man can co-operate with this system, building and contributing to it, or do the reverse and cause destruction even of things already in existence. From this premise it follows that a man's term of life on this earth is just long enough for him to fulfill his purpose; neither a day too short nor a day too long. Hence, if a person should permit a single day, or week, let alone months, to pass by without his fulfilling his purpose, it is an irretrievable loss for him and for the universal system at large.

The physical world as a whole, as can be seen clearly from man's physical body in particular, is not something independent and separate from the spiritual world and soul. In other words, we have not here two separate spheres of influence as the pagans used to think, rather we are now conscious of a unifying force which controls the universal system which we call monotheism. For this reason it is possible to understand many things about the soul from parallels with the physical body.

The physical body requires a daily intake of certain elements in certain quantities obtained through breathing and consuming food. No amount of thinking, speaking and studying about these elements can substitute for the actual intake of air and food. All this knowledge will not add one iota of health to the body unless it is given its required physical sustenance; on the contrary, the denial of the actual intake of the required elements will weaken the mental forces of thought and concentration. Thus it is obvious that the proper approach to ensure the health of the body is not by way of study first and practice afterwards but the reverse, to eat and drink and breathe which, in turn, will strengthen the mental powers.

Similarly, the soul and the elements which it requires daily for its sustenance are known best to its Creator. A healthy soul is first and foremost attained by the performance of mitzvoth, and understanding of them may come later.

The lesson from all the above is clear enough. For a person, every day that passes without living according to the Torah involves an irretrievable loss for him and for all humankind, inasmuch as we all form a single unity and are mutually responsible for one another. It also has an effect on the universal order and any theories attempting to justify it cannot alter this in the least.

HERE ARE SOME POINTS TO PONDER

Can I be a good person without believing in G-d?

What is the Divine Bridge?

What is the ultimate happiness?

What is the true meaning of good?

The Torah is life for every one?

Acts of goodness & kindness as G-d is

CHAPTER - 10

REDEMPTION – THE REAL WORLD

W hat is the Jewish Belief About 'The End of Days'?

The term "End of Days" is taken from Numbers 24:4. This has always been taken as a reference to the messianic era and therefore we shall explore – albeit briefly – the Jewish belief in the coming of Mashiach, messiah.

What does the word Mashiach mean? Mashiach is the Hebrew word for Messiah. The word Messiah in English means a saviour or a "hoped-for deliverer". The word Mashiach in Hebrew actually means "anointed". In Biblical Hebrew the title Mashiach was bestowed on somebody who had attained a position of nobility and greatness. For example, the High Priest is referred to as the Kohen Hamashiach.

In Talmudic literature the title Mashiach, or Melech Hamashiach, (the King Messiah) is reserved for the Jewish leader who will redeem Israel in the End of Days.

WHAT IS THE BELIEF IN MASHIACH?

One of the principles of Jewish faith enumerated by Maimonides is that one day there will arise a dynamic Jewish leader, a direct descendant of the Davidic dynasty, who will rebuild the Temple in Jerusalem and gather Jews from all over the world and bring them back to the Land of Israel.

All the nations of the world will recognize Mashiach to be a world leader and will accept his dominion. In the messianic era there will be world peace, no more wars nor famine and, in general, a high standard of living.

All mankind will worship one G–d and live a more spiritual and moral way of life. The Jewish nation will be preoccupied with learning Torah and fathoming its secrets.

The coming of Mashiach will complete G–d's purpose in creation: for man to make an dwelling place for G–d in the lower worlds; to reveal the inherent spirituality in the material world.

IS THIS NOT A UTOPIAN DREAM?

No! Judaism fervently believes that, with the correct leadership, humankind can and will change for the better. The leadership quality of Mashiach means that through his dynamic personality and example, coupled with his manifest humility, he will inspire all people to strive for good. He will transform a seemingly utopian dream into a reality. He will be recognised as a man of G–d with greater leadership qualities than even Moshe.

In today's society many people are repulsed by the breakdown of ethical and moral standards. Life is cheap, crime is rampant, drug and alcohol abuse are on the increase, and children have lost respect for their elders. At the same time technology has advanced in quantum leaps. There is no doubt that today, if channeled correctly, man has all the resources necessary to create a good standard of living for all mankind. He lacks only the social and political will. Mashiach will inspire all men to fulfill that aim.

WHY THE BELIEF IN A HUMAN MESSIAH?

Some people believe that the world will "evolve" by itself into a messianic era without a human figurehead. Judaism rejects this belief. Human history has been dominated by empire builders greedy for power.

Others believe in Armageddon – that the world will self-destruct, either by nuclear war or by terrorism. Again Judaism rejects this view.

Our prophets speak of the advent of a human leader, the magnitude of whom the world has not yet experienced. His unique example and leadership will inspire mankind to change direction.

Where is Mashiach mentioned in the Scriptures? The Scriptures are replete with messianic quotes. In Deuteronomy 30:1 Moshe prophesies that, after the Jews have been scattered to the four corners of the earth, there will come a time when they will repent and return to Israel where they will fulfil all the commandments of the Torah. The gentile prophet Bilam prophesies that this return will be lead by Mashiach (see Numbers 24:17-20). Jacob refers to Mashiach by the name Shilo (Genesis 49:10).

The prophets Isaiah, Jeremiah, Ezekiel, Amos, Joel and Hosea all refer to the messianic era. It is interesting to note that on the wall of the United Nations building in New York is inscribed the quote from Isaiah (Ch.11:6), "And the wolf shall lie with the lamb". Furthermore, it is clear from the prophets, when studied in their original Hebrew, that Mashiach is a Jewish concept and will entail return to Torah law, firmly ruling out any "other" messianic belief.

What sort of leader will Mashiach be? Mashiach will be a man who possesses extraordinary qualities. He will be proficient in both the written and oral Torah traditions. He will incessantly campaign for Torah observance among Jews and observance of the Seven Universal Noahide Laws by non-Jews. He will be scrupulously observant and encourage the highest standards from others. He will defend religious principles and repair breaches in their observance. Above all, Mashiach will be heralded as a true Jewish King, a person who leads the way in the service of G–d, totally humble yet enormously inspiring.

WHEN WILL MASHIACH COME?

Jews anticipate the arrival of Mashiach everyday. Our prayers are full of requests to G–d to usher in the messianic era. Even at the gates of the gas chambers many Jews sang, "Ani Maamin" – I believe in the coming of Mashiach!

However, the Talmud states that there is a predestined time when Mashiach will come. If we are meritorious he may come even before that predestined time. This "end of time" remains a mystery, yet the Talmud states that it will be before the Hebrew year 6000.

This does not rule out the possibility of Mashiach coming today and now if we merit it. It should be noted that many Torah authorities are of the opinion that we are in the "epoch of the Mashiach" and the Lubavitcher Rebbe stated on numerous occasions that the messianic redemption is imminent.

COULD MASHIACH COME AT ANY TIME IN ANY GENERATION?

Yes. In every generation there is a person who potentially could be the Mashiach. When G–d decides the time has arrived, He will bestow upon that individual the necessary powers for him to precipitate that redemption.

Any potential Mashiach must be a direct descendant of King David as well as erudite in Torah learning. It should be noted that many people living today can trace their lineage back to King David. The Chief Rabbi of Prague in the 16th Century, Rabbi Yehuda Loew (the Maharal), had a family tree that traced him back to the Davidic dynasty. Consequently, any direct descendant of the Maharal is of Davidic descent.

Maimonides, a great Jewish philosopher and codifier of the 12th Century, rules that if we recognise a human being who possesses the superlative qualities ascribed to Mashiach we may presume that he is the potential Mashiach. If this individual actually succeeds in rebuilding the Temple and gathering in the exiles then he is the Mashiach.

WHAT EXACTLY WILL HAPPEN WHEN MASHIACH COMES?

Maimonides states in his Mishnah Torah – a compendium of the entire halachic tradition – that Mashiach will first rebuild the Temple and then gather in the exiles. Jerusalem and the Temple will be the focus of Divine worship and "From Zion shall go forth Torah, and the word of the L–rd from Jerusalem."

The Sanhedrin – a supreme Jewish law court of 71 sages – will be established and will decide on all matters of law. At this time all Jews will return to full Torah observance and practice. It should be noted that in this present age of great assimilation and emancipation an unprecedented return of Jews to true Torah values has taken place. This "Baal Teshuvah" phenomenon is on the increase and paves the way for a full return in the messianic era.

Will miracles happen? The Talmud discusses this question and again arrives at the conclusion that, if we are meritorious, the messianic redemption will be accompanied by miracles. However, the realization of the messianic dream, even if it takes place naturally, will be the greatest miracle.

According to some traditions G–d Himself will rebuild the third Temple. According to others it will be rebuilt by Mashiach, while others suggest a combination of the two opinions. Some suggest that there will be two distinct periods in the messianic era: the first, a non-miraculous period, leading on to a second miraculous period.

Maimonides writes, "Neither the order of the occurrence of these events nor their precise detail is among the fundamental principles of the faith ... one should wait and believe in the general conception of the matter."

WHAT WILL BECOME OF THE WORLD AS WE KNOW IT?

Initially, there will be no change in the world order other than its readiness to accept messianic rule. All the nations of the world will strive to create a new world order in which there will be no more wars or conflicts. Jealousy, hatred, greed and political strife (of the negative kind) will disappear and all human beings will strive only for good, kindness and peace.

In the messianic era there will be great advances in technology allowing a high standard of living. Food will be plentiful and cheap.

However the focus of human aspiration will be the pursuit of the "knowledge of G–d." People will become less materialistic and more spiritual.

WHAT CAN BE DONE TO BRING MASHIACH?

In general, mankind must strive to perform more acts of goodness and kindness. Every person is mandated to learn and be aware of the messianic redemption, and strengthen his faith in Mashiach's ultimate and imminent arrival.

Charity is a catalyst for redemption and every day in our prayers we sincerely plead many times for the rebuilding of Jerusalem, the in-gathering of the exiles and the return to Torah observance under the leadership of Mashiach. The Lubavitcher Rebbe mounted a worldwide Mashiach campaign to heighten the awareness of Mashiach's imminent arrival. The Rebbe constantly urged every person to prepare himself, his family and his community for the arrival of Mashiach. This can best be achieved by "living with Mashiach"; that is, by learning about Mashiach and yearning for his coming.

In particular, each person has been charged with his/her own personal mission, to reveal G-dliness in his/her own portion of the world. Since this mission is associated with the ultimate purpose of the refinement of the world, our souls cannot be fulfilled until we have completed this task. When a person isolates himself from involvement within the world, even if he devotes himself to a life of study and prayer, he ignores this fundamental G-dly intent.

What good are the spiritual heights he will attain, if G-d's will has not been fulfilled? The goal for which a person should strive is not his individual refinement alone, but rather, the refinement of the entire world.

Surely, involvement with worldly matters presents a challenge, creating the possibility for self-indulgence and spiritual decline. Nevertheless, by remaining conscious of the purpose for which G-d sent us to exile, we can overcome that challenge and achieve both spiritual and material success.

Just as the many years of servitude in Egypt were necessary stages in the process that led to the exodus, similarly the present exile has as its purpose the ultimate Redemption. Since, in the Era of the Redemption, G-dliness will be revealed in all places and in all things, the service that prepares for that revelation must likewise be all-inclusive. Hence, our people have been spread throughout the world and have become involved in every aspect of existence.

Ultimately, each individual's efforts in making his/her environment a dwelling place for G-d, will prepare the entire world for the era when "the earth will be filled with the knowledge of G-d, as the waters cover the ocean bed."

HERE ARE SOME POINT TO PONDER.

Can Mashiach, messiah come anytime?

What will become of the world as we know it?

What will this world be like – start living it today.

All will come to know and praise G-d as his name will be one.

The world will be filled with Divine knowledge as the light of G-d will shine.

Giving charity and doing good deeds will bring the era of Mashiach.

EDUCATION DAY U.S.A

PUBLIC LAW 102-14, H.J. RES 104 102ND CONGRESS OF THE UNITED STATES OF AMERICA

Whereas Congress recognizes the historical tradition of ethical values and principles which are the basis of civilized society and upon which our great Nation was founded;

Whereas these ethical values and principles have been the bedrock of society from the dawn of civilization, when they were known as the Seven Noahide Laws;

Whereas without these ethical values and principles the edifice of civilization stands in serious peril of returning to chaos;

Whereas society is profoundly concerned with the recent weakening of these principles that has resulted in crises that beleaguer and threaten the fabric of civilized society;

Whereas the justified preoccupation with these crises must not let the citizens of this Nation lose sight of their responsibility to transmit these historical ethical values from our distinguished past to the generations of the future;

Whereas the Lubavitch movement has fostered and promoted these ethical values and principles throughout the world;

Whereas Rabbi Menachem Mendel Schneerson, leader of the Lubavitch movement, is universally respected and revered and his eighty-ninth birthday falls on March 26, 1991;

Whereas in tribute to this great spiritual leader, "the Rebbe," this, his ninetieth year will be seen as one of "education and giving," the year in which we turn to education and charity to return the world to the moral and ethical values contained in the Seven Noahide Laws; and

Whereas this will be reflected in an international scroll of honor signed by the President of the United States and other heads of state: Now, therefore, be it

Resolved by the Senate and House of Representatives of the United States of America in Congress assembled, That March 26, 1991, the start of the ninetieth year of Rabbi Menachem Schneerson, leader of the worldwide Lubavitch movement, is designated as Education Day U.S.A The President is requested to issue a proclamation calling upon the people of the United States to observe such day with appropriate ceremonies and activities.

Approved March 20, 1991.

Signed by George Bush,

President of the United States of America

GLOSSARY

Baal Shem Tov – Lit. "Master of a good name" – a reference to Rabbi Israel ben Eliezer, the founder of the chassidic movement.

Chabad – An acrostic formed from the initial letters of the words Chochmah, (wisdom), Bina, (comprehension), Da'at (knowledge). Generally used to describe the intellectual approach of the Chabad,Lubavitch movement.

Chassid – (plural: chassidim): Follower of the Rebbe, adherent of the chassidic life style.

Chassidut – chassidic philosophy.

Halachah – Torah law.

Hashem – G–d.

Kabbalah – "Inner" esoteric depths of Torah; mysticism.

Lubavitch – a town in White Russia, centre of the Chabad-Lubavitch movement. **Mashiach** – Messiah.

Mishnah – the earliest compilation of the Oral tradition.

Mitzvah (plur: mitzvot) – Precept or command of Torah.

Moshe – Moses.

Neshamah – Soul.

Rebbe – leader and head of the chassidim.

Shechinah – Divine Presence.

Talmud – a voluminous compendium of Torah oral tradition.

Tanya – Source text of Chabad; written by Rabbi Shneur Zalman of Liadi (1745-1812).

Torah – The overall body of Jewish religious teachings; scriptural and rabbinic.

Tzedakah – Charity.

Printed in Great Britain
by Amazon

71489187R00058